AF270658

PHILADELPHIA EAGLES

KENNY ABDO

Fly!
An Imprint of Abdo Zoom
abdobooks.com

abdobooks.com

Published by Abdo Zoom, a division of ABDO, P.O. Box 398166, Minneapolis, Minnesota 55439. Copyright © 2022 by Abdo Consulting Group, Inc. International copyrights reserved in all countries. No part of this book may be reproduced in any form without written permission from the publisher. Fly!™ is a trademark and logo of Abdo Zoom.

Printed in the United States of America, North Mankato, Minnesota.
052021
092021

Photo Credits: AP Images, Getty Images, Icon Sportswire, iStock, Shutterstock PREMIER
Production Contributors: Kenny Abdo, Jennie Forsberg, Grace Hansen
Design Contributors: Candice Keimig, Neil Klinepier

Library of Congress Control Number: 2020919700

Publisher's Cataloging-in-Publication Data

Names: Abdo, Kenny, author.
Title: Philadelphia Eagles / by Kenny Abdo
Description: Minneapolis, Minnesota : Abdo Zoom, 2022 | Series: NFL teams |
    Includes online resources and index.
Identifiers: ISBN 9781098224769 (lib. bdg.) | ISBN 9781098225704 (ebook) |
    ISBN 9781098226176 (Read-to-Me ebook)
Subjects: LCSH: Philadelphia Eagles (Football team)--Juvenile literature. | National
    Football League--Juvenile literature. | Football teams--Juvenile literature. |
    American football--Juvenile literature. | Professional sports--Juvenile literature.
Classification: DDC 796.33264--dc23

TABLE OF CONTENTS

PHILADELPHIA EAGLES

With a long, storied history, the Philadelphia Eagles have had many great players sport the black and green jerseys.

As the seventh-oldest NFL franchise, the Eagles have always displayed greatness with several trips to the playoffs and many Hall of Fame players.

The Eagles were founded in 1933 by Bert Bell and Lud Wray. The team started off strong by winning the 1948 and 1949 NFL **championships**!

Bert Bell

With mostly disappointing seasons in the 1950s, the Eagles swung back to beat the Green Bay Packers at the 1960 NFL **championship**!

With less than a minute remaining in a 1978 season game, Cornerback Herman Edwards recovered a fumble from the Giants, scoring a touchdown. The Eagles won the game by two points, leading the team to the playoffs for the first time in 18 years! It is known as the "Miracle at the Meadowlands."

TEAM RECAPS

The Eagles made their first appearance at **Super Bowl** XV in 1981. And they were favored to win by three points! Unfortunately, the Eagles lost to the Raiders 27–10.

The Eagles wouldn't play at the **Super Bowl** again until the 2004 season. Unfortunately, they lost the Super Bowl to the Patriots by just three points.

In week 14 of the 2017 season, **QB** Carson Wentz had a season ending injury. With the help of backup QB Nick Foles, the Eagles made it to **Super Bowl** LII. And they won! The Eagles beat the Patriots 41–33.

The Eagles had many players who suffered injuries throughout the 2019 season. They still won the **NFC** East division title! Sadly, they lost to the Seahawks 17–9 during the **Wild Card Round**.

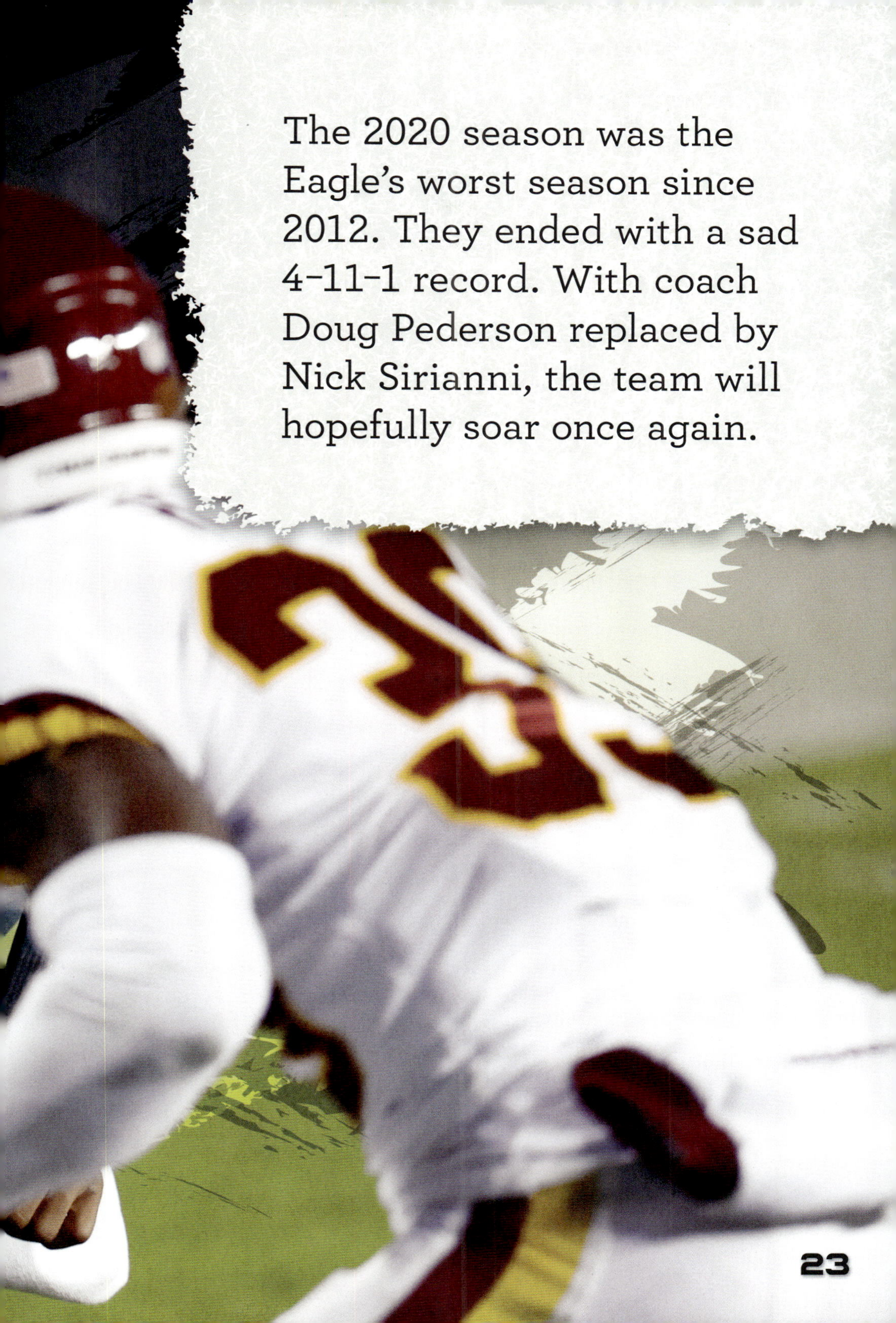

The 2020 season was the Eagle's worst season since 2012. They ended with a sad 4-11-1 record. With coach Doug Pederson replaced by Nick Sirianni, the team will hopefully soar once again.

HALL OF FAME

Halfback Steve Van Buren totaled 5,860 rushing yards and 523 receiving yards in his eight seasons as an Eagle. Van Buren became a member of the Pro Football Hall of Fame in 1965.

15
25

In his eleven years with the team, **QB** Donovan McNabb led the Eagles to four straight **NFC** East Division **championships**. He also helped the team make it to the **Super Bowl**. McNabb had 216 touchdowns and 32,873 yards passed with the team.

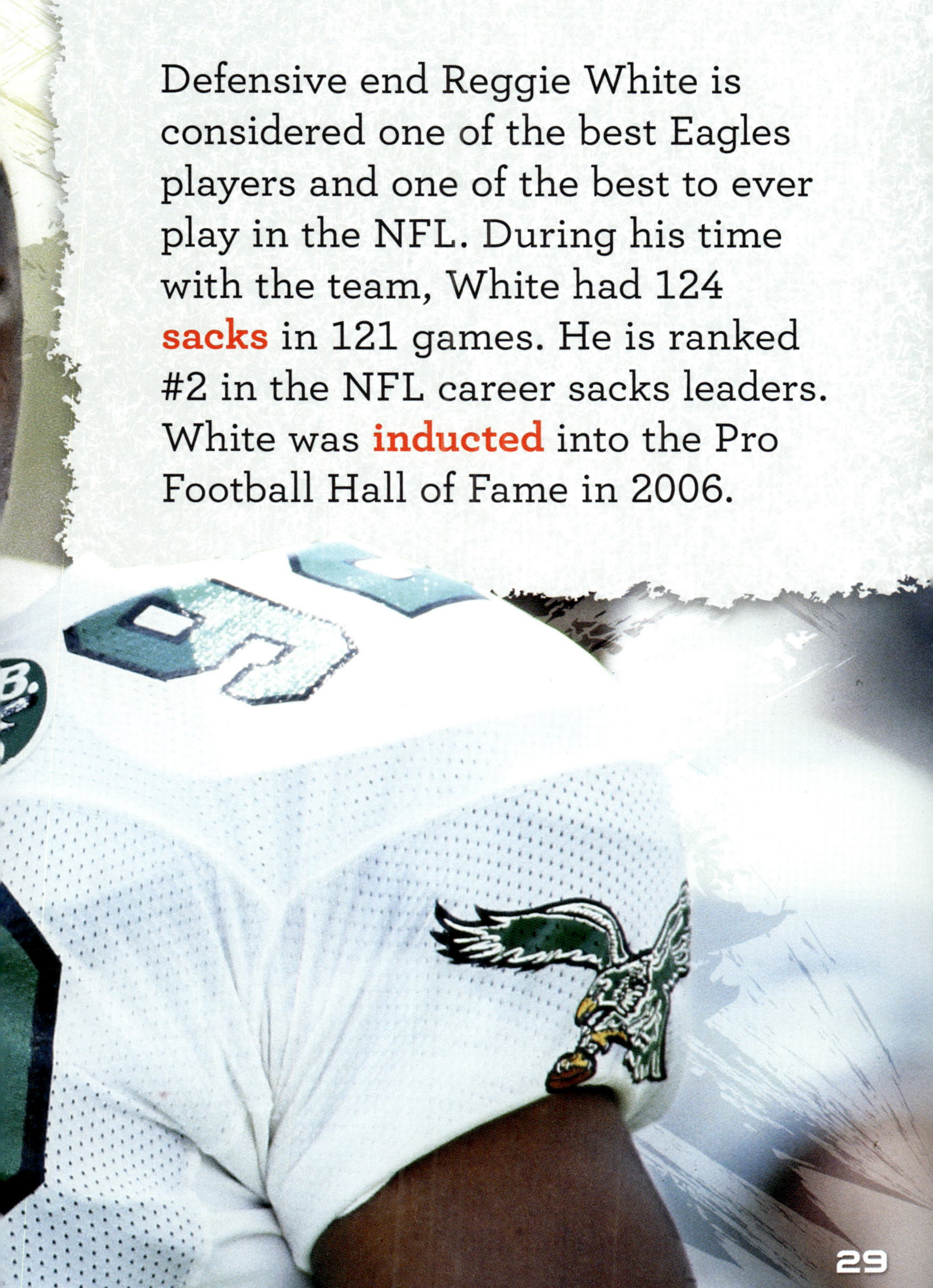

Defensive end Reggie White is considered one of the best Eagles players and one of the best to ever play in the NFL. During his time with the team, White had 124 **sacks** in 121 games. He is ranked #2 in the NFL career sacks leaders. White was **inducted** into the Pro Football Hall of Fame in 2006.

GLOSSARY

championship – a game held to find a first-place winner.

induct – to admit someone as a member of an organization.

National Football Conference (NFC) – one of two major conferences of the NFL. Each conference contains 16 teams split into four divisions. The winner of the NFC championship plays the AFC winner at the Super Bowl.

quarterback (QB) – the player on the offensive team that directs teammates in their play.

sack – when a quarterback is tackled behind the line of scrimmage while still in possession of the ball.

Super Bowl – the NFL championship game, played once a year.

Wild Card Round – the first round of the playoffs. Each of the two conferences send four division champions and three wild-card teams to its postseason.

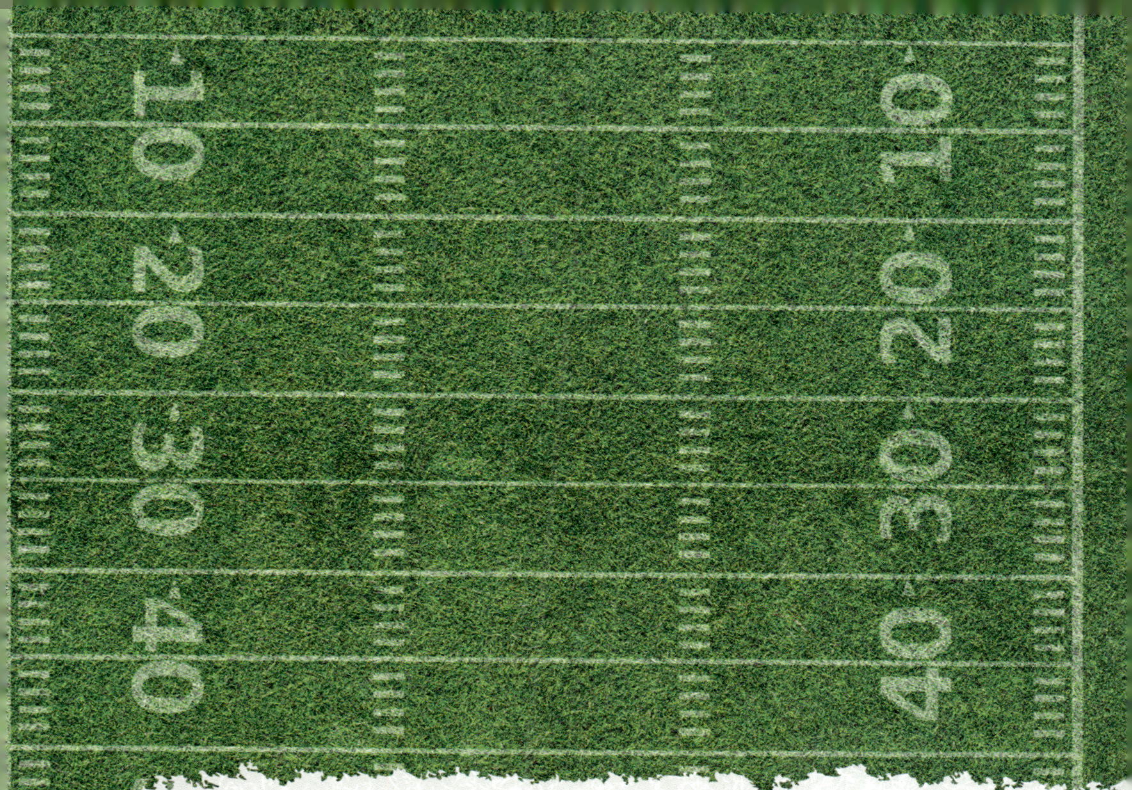

ONLINE RESOURCES

To learn more about the Philadelphia Eagles, please visit **abdobooklinks.com** or scan this QR code. These links are routinely monitored and updated to provide the most current information available.

INDEX